FARM MACHINES

PLOW

KATHY MIDDLETON

A Crabtree Roots Book

Crabtree Publishing
crabtreebooks.com

School-to-Home Support for Caregivers and Teachers

This book helps children grow by letting them practice reading. Here are a few guiding questions to help readers build comprehension skills. Possible answers appear here in red.

Before Reading:

- What do I think this book is about?
    - *I think this book is about plows.*
    - *I think this book will talk about what plows do.*
- What do I want to learn about this topic?
    - *I want to learn about what jobs plows do.*
    - *I want to learn why plows are important farm machines.*

During Reading:

- I wonder why...
    - *I wonder why farmers use tractors.*
    - *I wonder why plows are needed on the farm.*
- What have I learned so far?
    - *I have learned that plows have blades.*
    - *I have learned that plows break up hard soil.*

After Reading:

- What details did I learn about this topic?
    - *I have learned that some plows attach to a tractor.*
    - *I learned that plows help prepare the ground for planting.*
- Read the book again and look for the vocabulary words.
    - *I see the words **plow** on page 3 and the word **soil** on page 4. The other vocabulary words are found on page 14.*

This is a **plow**.

A plow digs deep to break up hard soil on the **farm**.

NEW HOLLAND

Most plows attach to a **tractor**.

Some plows have metal **blades** that dig.

Soil looks dark brown and bumpy after plowing.

Plows get the ground ready for planting **crops**.

Word List

Sight Words

a	get	most	soil
attach	ground	metal	that
deep	have	on	the
digs	into	planting	this
for	is	ready	to

Words to Know

blades

crops

farm

plow

tractor

45 Words

This is a **plow**.

A plow digs deep to break up hard soil on the **farm**.

Most plows attach to a **tractor**.

Some plows have metal **blades** that dig.

Soil looks dark brown and bumpy after plowing.

Plows get the ground ready for planting **crops**.

FARM MACHINES PLOW

Written by: Kathy Middleton
Designed by: Under the Oaks Media
Proofreader: Crystal Sikkens
Production manager: Candice Campbell
Prepress technician: Katherine Kantor

Photographs: All images from Sutterstock

Crabtree Publishing

crabtreebooks.com 800-387-7650

In Canada: We acknowledge the financial support of the Government of Canada through the Canada Book Fund for our publishing activities.

Printed in the U.S.A./CP2025

Published in Canada
Crabtree Publishing
616 Welland Ave.
St. Catharines, Ontario
L2M 5V6

Published in the United States
Crabtree Publishing
347 Fifth Ave
Suite 1402-145
New York, NY 10016

Library and Archives Canada Cataloguing in Publication
Available at Library and Archives Canada

Library of Congress Cataloging-in-Publication Data
Available at the Library of Congress

Hardcover: 978-1-0398-8104-4
Paperback: 978-1-0398-8465-6
Ebook (pdf): 978-1-0398-8224-9
Epub: 978-1-0398-8344-4
Audio: 978-1-0398-8507-3
Read-Along: 978-1-0398-8549-3